This journal belongs to:

_____

*"RE-EXAMINE ALL YOU HAVE BEEN TOLD.
DISMISS WHAT INSULTS YOUR SOUL."*

Walt Whitman

The Self-Exploration Journal

Follow us on Instagram

For promotions, giveaways and newest arrivals

Instagram: 21exercises_journals

A Message From The Authors

Journaling is a way to better understand life, the people around you and yourself. It's a peaceful exercise that demands us to hold still for a brief moment, escaping clouded Facebook feeds, screaming news channels and daily stress.

An ancient exercise, also, to think about life. Recharging your battery. Setting a new direction. And, above all, being conscious, living in the here and now, open to new experiences, able to connect with others and reassured of your ability to cope with (temporary) setbacks.

Dear Reader,

Thanks for purchasing our book.

We feel grateful to serve you with our carefully created:

The Self-Exploration Journal

& Hope you enjoy, learn and find what you're looking for.

All the best,

21 Exercises

As a little thank you note,
*we've three **FREE** Personal-Growth exercises waiting for you.*

Simply send an email to to exercises21@yahoo.com
Title the email "The Self-Exploration Journal"

And we will send you Three Personal Development Hacks for FREE.

The Self-Exploration Journal

---

90 Days of Writing, Discovery & Reflection

Created by:
21 EXERCISES

Introduction

Question

noun

kwes.tʃən

A SENTENCE WORDED OR EXPRESSED SO AS TO ELICIT INFORMATION.

This 90-day workbook is designed to send you on a journey of self-exploration. It offers thought-provoking questions about goals, health, love, self-acceptance and much, much more, to let you think about your own life. Better questions lead to better answers. Better answers lead to a better life.

How To Use This Journal

On every page, you'll find a new day and a new question. If you bought the print version, there is enough space on each page to answer the question and do some more journaling. If you bought the EBook version, you could use your own notebook during these 90 days. We recommend setting a particular time each day for your journaling exercises; for example during your morning routine, or before you go to bed..

EVERY HEART SINGS A SONG, INCOMPLETE, UNTIL ANOTHER HEART
WHISPERS BACK. THOSE WHO WISH TO SING ALWAYS FIND A SONG.
AT THE TOUCH OF A LOVER, EVERYONE BECOMES A POET.

PLATO

Day 1

"FOR IT IS IN YOUR POWER TO RETIRE INTO YOURSELF WHENEVER YOU CHOOSE."

Marcus Aurelius

What is the main reason you feel the need to go on this journey of self-discovery?

Day 2

Write down a list of thoughts that you frequently have
that only bring you stress and unhappiness?
What would be the best way to deal with these thoughts?

Day 3

"WHAT IS THAT YOU EXPRESS IN YOUR EYES?
IT SEEMS TO ME MORE THAN ALL THE PRINT I HAVE READ IN MY LIFE."

Walt Whitman

Describe the last time you overcame a difficult period in your life.
What lessons can you learn from that?

Day 4

Deep down, what do you know is your mission here on earth?

_____
_____
_____
_____
_____
_____
_____
_____
_____
_____
_____
_____
_____
_____
_____
_____
_____
_____
_____
_____
_____
_____
_____
_____
_____
_____
_____
_____
_____
_____

Day 5

If today you had all the courage in the world,
what three actions would you take?

_____

_____

_____

_____

_____

_____

_____

_____

_____

_____

_____

_____

_____

_____

_____

_____

_____

_____

_____

_____

_____

_____

_____

_____

Day 6

Write down three experiences from the past that had a life-changing influence on your love life.

Day 7

Imagine you would meet yourself today in a bar.
What one advice would you give to yourself?

_____
_____
_____
_____
_____
_____
_____
_____
_____
_____
_____
_____
_____
_____
_____
_____
_____
_____
_____
_____
_____
_____
_____
_____
_____
_____
_____
_____
_____

Day 8

**"GIVEN THE CHOICE BETWEEN THE EXPERIENCE OF PAIN AND NOTHING,
I WOULD CHOOSE PAIN."**

William Faulkner, *The Wild Palms*

What experience from the past is still running your life in a negative way?
What can you do to heal this experience?

_____

_____

_____

_____

_____

_____

_____

_____

_____

_____

_____

_____

_____

_____

_____

_____

_____

_____

_____

_____

_____

_____

_____

_____

_____

_____

Day 9

Write down 5 things you have done in recent years
that makes you feel proud.

Day 10

**"I'M NOT STRANGE, WEIRD, OFF, NOR CRAZY,
MY REALITY IS JUST DIFFERENT FROM YOURS."**

Lewis Carroll

Write down all the negative things you associate with money. Then look at the list. How do these thoughts affect your current money situation?

Day 11

If people knew this about me, they would better understand me....

_____

_____

_____

_____

_____

_____

_____

_____

_____

_____

_____

_____

_____

_____

_____

_____

_____

_____

_____

_____

_____

_____

_____

_____

_____

_____

_____

_____

Day 12

William Shakespeare, *As You Like It*

What are you chasing in life?
How can you attract this into your life, without chasing it?

_____

_____

_____

_____

_____

_____

_____

_____

_____

_____

_____

_____

_____

_____

_____

_____

_____

_____

_____

_____

_____

_____

_____

_____

_____

Day 13

Write down three fears
that block you from experiencing the love life you would like to have.

_____

_____

_____

_____

_____

_____

_____

_____

_____

_____

_____

_____

_____

_____

_____

_____

_____

_____

_____

_____

_____

_____

_____

_____

_____

_____

_____

_____

_____

_____

Day 14

Write down a compelling list (20 or more)
of all the things you're grateful for in your life.

Day 15

What new aspects about yourself have you noticed over the past few months?

_____
_____
_____
_____
_____
_____
_____
_____
_____
_____
_____
_____
_____
_____
_____
_____
_____
_____
_____
_____
_____
_____
_____
_____
_____
_____
_____
_____

Day 16

Imagine you earn twice as much money per month than you earn right now. How would you spend it? Make an exact budget on how to spend this money.

Day 17

Write down all the positive things you associate with money.

_____
_____
_____
_____
_____
_____
_____
_____
_____
_____
_____
_____
_____
_____
_____
_____
_____
_____
_____
_____
_____
_____
_____
_____
_____
_____
_____
_____
_____
_____

Day 18

**"HOW CAN YOU WASTE TIME? YOU HAVE ONLY SO MUCH TO USE,
AND NO MATTER WHAT YOU DO, IT STILL PASSES."**

Felix Salten

Who is your role model? What qualities do you admire in her or him?

Day 19

If you no longer had to worry about money, what would you be doing?

Day 20

How can the fear based news projected in the media,
affect your life negatively?

_____
_____
_____
_____
_____
_____
_____
_____
_____
_____
_____
_____
_____
_____
_____
_____
_____
_____
_____
_____
_____
_____
_____
_____
_____
_____

Day 21

Are you a giver or a taker in your personal relationships?
What has been the result of that?

Day 22

"IT IS THE MARK OF AN EDUCATED MIND TO BE ABLE TO ENTERTAIN A THOUGHT
WITHOUT ACCEPTING IT."

Aristotle, *Metaphysics*

How would you describe yourself?

Day 23

How would the people closest to you describe you?

Day 24

"THE UNEXAMINED LIFE IS NOT WORTH LIVING."

Socrates

When did you last laugh so much that it hurt?

Day 25

**"THE SIMPLE THINGS ARE ALSO THE MOST EXTRAORDINARY THINGS,
AND ONLY THE WISE CAN SEE THEM."**

Paulo Coelho, *The Alchemist*

Write down one of your best childhood memories.

Day 26

Write down three experiences from the past that had a life-changing influence on how you see yourself.

Day 27

Write down at least twelve things you like about yourself.

Day 28

"BY THREE METHODS WE MAY LEARN WISDOM: FIRST, BY REFLECTION,
WHICH IS NOBLEST; SECOND, BY IMITATION, WHICH IS EASIEST;
AND THIRD BY EXPERIENCE, WHICH IS THE BITTEREST."

Confucius

What book changed your life the most? Why?

Day 29

What is your body trying to tell you over the past few weeks?

Day 30

How much time do you spend each day thinking about the past or worrying about/making plans for the future?

Day 31

What can other people learn from you?

_____
_____
_____
_____
_____
_____
_____
_____
_____
_____
_____
_____
_____
_____
_____
_____
_____
_____
_____
_____
_____
_____
_____
_____
_____
_____
_____

Day 32

"ATTENTION IS THE RAREST AND PUREST FORM OF GENEROSITY."

Simone Weil

Do you take care of yourself as well as you take care of others?
Why or why not?

Day 33

Imagine you would talk with your future self. A version of you ten years from now. What would he or she say to you?

Day 34

"IT TAKES SOMETHING MORE THAN INTELLIGENCE TO ACT INTELLIGENTLY."

Fyodor Dostoyevsky, *Crime and Punishment*

What is your best memory from the last few years?

Day 35

When was the last time you said 'yes' when you really wanted to say no?
Why?

Day 36

"LANGUAGE IS THE LIGHT OF THE MIND."

John Stuart Mill

When was the last time you said 'no' when you really wanted to say yes?
Why?

_____

_____

_____

_____

_____

_____

_____

_____

_____

_____

_____

_____

_____

_____

_____

_____

_____

_____

_____

_____

_____

_____

_____

_____

_____

Day 37

Write down a list of activities that always makes you feel good.

Day 38

**"I HAVE NEVER MET A MAN SO IGNORANT
THAT I COULDN'T LEARN SOMETHING FROM HIM."**

Galileo Galilei

Write down the people in your life that have a positive influence on you.
And write down the people in your life that have a negative influence on you.

_____
_____
_____
_____
_____
_____
_____
_____
_____
_____
_____
_____
_____
_____
_____
_____
_____
_____
_____
_____
_____
_____
_____
_____
_____
_____
_____
_____

Day 39

Fanny Fern

How would you treat the planet if it was a conscious living being?

Day 40

Write down three experiences from the past that had a life-changing influence on how you deal with money.

Day 41

"SOMETIMES IT'S NOT ENOUGH TO KNOW WHAT THINGS MEAN,
SOMETIMES YOU HAVE TO KNOW WHAT THINGS DON'T MEAN."

Bob Dylan

Write down at least twelve things
that makes you an attractive person to be around.

Day 42

What is your definition of success?

Day 43

What is the next better version of you?

Day 44

"A VERY IMPORTANT THING IS NOT TO MAKE UP YOUR MIND THAT YOU ARE ANY ONE THING."

Gertrude Stein

When was the last time your mind stopped your intuition?
What was the reason for it?

Day 45

What mistakes do you constantly repeat when it comes to your love life?
How can you avoid these mistakes in the future?

Day 46

"WORDS ARE BUT THE VAGUE SHADOWS OF THE VOLUMES WE MEAN.
LITTLE AUDIBLE LINKS, THEY ARE,
CHAINING TOGETHER GREAT INAUDIBLE FEELINGS AND PURPOSES."

Theodore Dreiser

What mistakes do you constantly repeat when it comes to your health?
How can you avoid these mistakes in the future?

Day 47

If you died today, what would you regret not seeing?

_____
_____
_____
_____
_____
_____
_____
_____
_____
_____
_____
_____
_____
_____
_____
_____
_____
_____
_____
_____
_____
_____
_____
_____
_____
_____
_____

Day 48

**"FAR BETTER IT IS TO DARE MIGHTY THINGS, TO WIN GLORIOUS TRIUMPHS, EVEN
THOUGH CHECKERED BY FAILURE, THAN TO TAKE RANK WITH THOSE POOR
SPIRITS WHO NEITHER ENJOY MUCH NOR SUFFER MUCH, BECAUSE THEY LIVE IN
THE GRAY TWILIGHT THAT KNOWS NEITHER VICTORY NOR DEFEAT."**

Theodore Roosevelt, *Strenuous Life*

What is your Inner Voice trying to tell you in the last few months?

_____
_____
_____
_____
_____
_____
_____
_____
_____
_____
_____
_____
_____
_____
_____
_____
_____
_____
_____
_____
_____
_____
_____
_____

Day 49

Who are the most important people in your life?
When was the last time you told them this?

Day 50

**"WHERE WISDOM REIGNS,
THERE IS NO CONFLICT BETWEEN THINKING AND FEELING."**

Carl Gustav Jung

Look in the mirror now, for three minutes straight. Set an alarm.
Try not to stare, but to look. Then, reflect on it. What did you see?

_____

_____

_____

_____

_____

_____

_____

_____

_____

_____

_____

_____

_____

_____

_____

_____

_____

_____

_____

_____

_____

_____

_____

_____

_____

Day 51

Based on your daily routines and actions,
how will your life look like one year from now?

_____
_____
_____
_____
_____
_____
_____
_____
_____
_____
_____
_____
_____
_____
_____
_____
_____
_____
_____
_____
_____
_____
_____
_____
_____
_____

Day 52

"WE ARE LIKE ISLANDS IN THE SEA, SEPARATE ON THE SURFACE
BUT CONNECTED IN THE DEEP."

William James

What is your most powerful habit? What about it is making it so powerful?

Day 53

What one simple action can you take this week to improve your relationship
with yourself? Describe exactly how you're going to do it.

_____

_____

_____

_____

_____

_____

_____

_____

_____

_____

_____

_____

_____

_____

_____

_____

_____

_____

_____

_____

_____

_____

_____

_____

_____

_____

_____

_____

Day 54

"DO ANYTHING, BUT LET IT PRODUCE JOY."

Walt Whitman

What are the three main reasons for your feelings of unhappiness?

_____

_____

_____

_____

_____

_____

_____

_____

_____

_____

_____

_____

_____

_____

_____

_____

_____

_____

_____

_____

_____

_____

_____

_____

_____

_____

_____

_____

_____

Day 55

What is your definition of love?

_____

_____

_____

_____

_____

_____

_____

_____

_____

_____

_____

_____

_____

_____

_____

_____

_____

_____

_____

_____

_____

_____

_____

_____

_____

_____

_____

_____

Day 56

**"YOU CANNOT TEACH A MAN ANYTHING,
YOU CAN ONLY HELP HIM FIND IT WITHIN HIMSELF."**

Galileo

Suppose your body is a temple,
what are some ways to take better care of it over the coming month?

Day 57

. What do you consider the character traits of a good friend?

Day 58

"WHAT DESTROYS US MOST EFFECTIVELY IS NOT A MALIGN FATE BUT OUR OWN CAPACITY FOR SELF-DECEPTION AND FOR DEGRADING OUR OWN BEST SELF."

George Eliot

When was the last time you did something impulsive?
What was the outcome?

Day 59

What feelings and thoughts are you suppressing?
What would happen with these feelings and thoughts in a year
if you don't give yourself the space to express them?

Day 60

"THE QUESTION IS NOT WHAT YOU LOOK AT, BUT WHAT YOU SEE."

Henry David Thoreau

What is your favorite way to deal with social anxiety?
What is a better way to deal with it?

Day 61

Write down at least seven things you find physically attractive about yourself.

Day 62

What has been the best advice you have received this year?

Day 63

Write down at least three new things you would like to try this year.

Day 64

"BUT THE FUTURE MUST BE MET, HOWEVER STERN AND IRON IT BE. "

Elizabeth Gaskell

If you could start your life over and change one thing,
what would you change? Why?

Day 65

What you would love to say to your family?

_____
_____
_____
_____
_____
_____
_____
_____
_____
_____
_____
_____
_____
_____
_____
_____
_____
_____
_____
_____
_____
_____
_____
_____
_____
_____
_____
_____
_____
_____

Day 66

**"THE UNIVERSE IS CHANGE;
OUR LIFE IS WHAT OUR THOUGHTS MAKE IT."**

Marcus Aurelius

What is the one thing you want to learn before you die?
What's stopping you from learning it now?

Day 67

What small steps can you take in the next month to improve your health?

Day 68

"Sorrow looks back, Worry looks around, Faith looks up"

Ralph Waldo Emerson

Twenty-five years from now, looking back on your life,
what do you think will matter most to you?

Day 69

What is your favorite way to deal with boredom?
What are three better ways to deal with it?

Day 70

**"THAT IT WILL NEVER COME AGAIN
IS WHAT MAKES LIFE SO SWEET."**

Emily Dickinson

What do you find most difficult about your relationship with yourself?
Write down one way to improve this.

Day 71

If you could eliminate one thing from your life today, what would it be? Why?

Day 72

"**DON'T GO AROUND SAYING THE WORLD OWES YOU A LIVING.
THE WORLD OWES YOU NOTHING. IT WAS HERE FIRST.**"

Mark Twain

Write down a compelling list (7 or more) of things you're fascinated by
when it comes to loving relationships.

Day 73

Is there a better version of you trying to climb out?
What is blocking it?

Day 74

**"A FAITHFUL FRIEND IS A STRONG DEFENSE;
AND HE THAT HATH FOUND HIM HATH FOUND A TREASURE."**

Louisa May Alcott

What would be the 7-year old version of you, think about you today?

Day 75

What reward(s) are you seeking in your life and why?

Day 76

**"DO NOT GIVE WAY TO USELESS ALARM;
THOUGH IT IS RIGHT TO BE PREPARED FOR THE WORST,
THERE IS NO OCCASION TO LOOK ON IT AS CERTAIN."**

Jane Austen

How does the image you hold up to the world
differ from your authentic self?

Day 77

What steps can you take in the next month
to improve your financial situation?

_____

_____

_____

_____

_____

_____

_____

_____

_____

_____

_____

_____

_____

_____

_____

_____

_____

_____

_____

_____

_____

_____

_____

_____

_____

_____

_____

Day 78

"FOREVER IS COMPOSED OF NOWS."

Emily Dickinson

If you were granted one wish of any kind, what would you wish for?

Day 79

What kind of people often make you feel insecure? Why?

Day 80

"LOSING YOUR WAY ON A JOURNEY IS UNFORTUNATE.
BUT, LOSING YOUR REASON FOR THE JOURNEY IS A FATE MORE CRUEL."

H.G. Wells

What would happen if you did everything the opposite
of how you normally do things for the next 24 hours?

Day 81

What is your favorite way of pleasing others? Is this behavior sincere?
Why or why not?

Day 82

In what area(s) of your life do you lack integrity? How come?

Day 83

"Realize that everything connects to everything else."

Leonardo Da Vinci

Write down three things you can do to express yourself authentically when it comes to your sex life.

_____

_____

_____

_____

_____

_____

_____

_____

_____

_____

_____

_____

_____

_____

_____

_____

_____

_____

_____

_____

_____

_____

_____

_____

_____

_____

_____

_____

_____

Day 84

What is hurting you deep inside? Take some time to answer this question,
dive into the feeling. Describe it in detail.

Day 85

**"ALL MEN WANT, NOT SOMETHING TO DO WITH,
BUT SOMETHING TO DO, OR RATHER SOMETHING TO BE."**

Henry David Thoreau

Look at the answer on the previous page. If you met this *hurt self* today, what
would he or she look like? What would he or she tell you?
What would you tell him or her?

Day 86

Who are you becoming?

Day 87

**"IF YOU LOOK THE RIGHT WAY,
YOU CAN SEE THAT THE WHOLE WORLD IS A GARDEN."**

Frances Hodgson Burnett

Write down a long list (at least twelve items) of all the things
you look forward to in the near future.

Day 88

What is your favorite way to deal with rejection?
What is a better way to deal with it?

Day 89

"LOVE IS THE ONLY THING THAT WE CAN CARRY WITH US WHEN WE GO,
AND IT MAKES THE END SO EASY."

Louisa May Alcott

What are the benefits of being patient?
How could you improve this in your own life?

Day 90

**"NEVER CLOSE YOUR LIPS TO THOSE
WHOM YOU HAVE ALREADY OPENED YOUR HEART."**

Charles Dickens

Write down all the reasons
why you deserve to live a happy and successful life.

Personal Journal

About 21 Exercises

We specialize in creating empowering, elegant & inspirational self-help journals. The power of journaling, of consistent self-reflection, is a scientifically proven habit that will benefit your life in truly astonishing ways. Mainly 90-Day or Yearly Journals, on various topics and for all types of people. Tools for self-reflection, gratitude & personal growth. We create each journal or workbook with the utmost care and the honest intention to give lasting benefit to our customers.

We hope to guide you through releasing limitations and discover your hidden potentials in all areas of life. And of course to give an enjoyable journaling experience. Step by step, to unlock the true you. Step by step, to a better world.

We'd love to hear your ideas, tips, and questions. Let us know at exercises21@yahoo.com

The Self-Exploration Journal

Follow us on Instagram

For promotions, giveaways and newest arrivals

Instagram: 21exercises_journals